INHERITANCE

Jasmine Cooray is a poet, psychotherapist and arts facilitator. She has been a Women of the World Festival speaker, BBC Performing Arts Fellow and Writer-in-Residence at the National University of Singapore, and has delivered creative writing projects for the Barbican, the Southbank Centre, First Story, the Arvon Foundation and the National Literacy Trust. Her pamphlet *Everything We Don't Say* was published by Tall Lighthouse in 2009. *Inheritance* is her first full collection of poetry.

BY THE SAME AUTHOR

Everything We Don't Say
(Tall Lighthouse, 2009)

Inheritance

JASMINE COORAY

BAD BETTY PRESS

First published in 2023 by Bad Betty Press
Cobden Place, Cobden Chambers, Nottingham NG1 2ED

badbettypress.com

Copyright © Jasmine Cooray 2023

Jasmine Cooray has asserted her right to be identified as the author of this work in accordance with Section 77 of the Copyright, Designs and Patents Act of 1988.

PB ISBN: 978-1-913268-50-3
EPUB ISBN: 978-1-913268-51-0

A CIP record of this book is available from the British Library.

Book design by Amy Acre

Printed and bound in the UK by TJ Books Limited, Padstow, Cornwall using FSC® Certified paper from responsibly managed forests

For Will

CONTENTS

Aurora Borealis

Aurora Borealis	13
Inventory	14
Now You Are Not Here to Leave Us	16
Visitor	17
Second Generation	18
Ice-Cream Box of Frozen Curry	20
How Not to Wrap a Saree	23
Fake Tan	25
Nasi Lemak with the Ancestors	26
Elders of the Pot	27
Quiet Men	28
I Am Not Going Anywhere I Promise	29

World of Wildflowers

Elegy for a Wedding	33
World of Wildflowers	34
The Fields	35
Inheritance	36
Blessing	37
Song for Absent Loves	38
The Call	40
Pack Everything Down	41
Portobello Dusk	42

Storyteller	43
Tawny Owl	44
Dream Posters	46

Sweet Milk

i – vi	49

Years That Ask Questions and Years That Answer

The Falling	59
A Taste of the End	60
Against the Grain	61
Sweet Prince	62
Badonk	63
Always the Quiet Ones	64
Making Amends	65
The Well	66
All the Trees Holding Hands Under the Earth	67
Bad Hosting	68
Years That Ask Questions and Years That Answer	70

Acknowledgements	72

Inheritance

AURORA BOREALIS

AURORA BOREALIS

I smuggled his ashes
across Norway in a soap box,

shook them into one hand, and threw.
The grain of him left my frozen palms,

rose into arctic air – icy jaws opening
to catch him – but some clung to my skin

as if he knew I didn't really want this
goodbye, this flame to a photograph.

I wanted his face to appear in the glow,
voice rumbling like Mufasa,

longed for him to speak from
the dizzying black: *I'm here, Baba.*

I kissed my palms, powder
lodged in fingerprint and lifeline.

I didn't yet know the ways
in which he would return,

cartwheel across the skies of me,
leave me shivering in his wake.

INVENTORY
after Breton

My father with malted Einstein hair
with hair of car-washed skunk
my father with brows of sand dunes
of amphitheatre seats
and his eyes like soft open oysters
eyes of wishing well coins
eyes of longline hooks
my father's eyes drilling to the centre of the earth
my father with cheeks of sandpaper
and ears of open hands
ears of flapping letterboxes
my father with shoulders like the hinges of industrial cranes
and his heart an enormous balloon
and his belly, a heavy coconut
a sack of coffee grounds
my father with marionette legs
legs of old door handles and rotten fruit
and his feet like rhino hide
feet of curled burning manuscript
of cracked city pavements
his voice a mountain echo
voice of butterfly flight
voice of wild salmon fighting current
and his laugh like a hard bristle brush on a front step
and his song a wayward supermarket trolley
a rabbit's foot necklace

a swishing ceremonial robe
my father's song a fading slideshow
and his hands like dry sea sponge
hands like giant open clams
my father's hands a magic porridge pot
refilling your bowl again.

NOW YOU ARE NOT HERE
TO LEAVE US

There are years that Ma will not talk about,
unwilling to look inside the decades that were

wooden cabinets riddled with exit holes.
She once said your other daughter, in her t-bar shoes,

would quieten at your goodbye kiss, then tether
herself to Ma's leg, rub her curly head against nylon

to hold at least one parent close with static.
The civil war hurtled you back and forth

over the oceans like a fire fought with a single bucket.
We learned how to wait, wobbled on a tightrope

of weeks, grooves bored so deep between foot
muscles that to descend at a key's turn in the lock

meant torn skin, blood. Now you are not here
to leave us, we privately tend our wounds

with bandages and arnica. We needed you,
we did. But when visitors come to hear stories

of the man in the mask and cape, we'll only
share proud tales, tight as tourniquets.

VISITOR
for Kayo Chingonyi

A couple walks past in the park – a dark man,
high waistband, seventy, a white woman

on his arm – and the other world where my father
is still alive slices past like a summer frisbee.

Another day, his reflection will turn up in a yolk,
a workers' caff where twenty-somethings in shades

drape limbs over Formica. *Can't beat egg and chips*,
his smile swimming like a light spot.

Later he'll float in to snag the gaze of my sister
as she walks the graduation stage, drift between

seats for a better view, blow his translucent nose.
He does this: sneaks up to change the slide,

and for a second the world still has him in it.
Afterwards, the face and jolt to the stomach

flood to another vault of the brain, days roll by,
trees hawk resin over cars, but he'll visit again,

a split-second bomb to the heart. Can't the city
around us see everything is a different colour now?

No child, it's only me, messing with the settings.

SECOND GENERATION

Inherit an ability to crawl behind the sun and wind it
an hour behind: buy time for that extra textbook chapter,

to slide from one grindstone to another. Funnel sleep
into a savings bond, though it will escape and bludgeon you

on public transport, at church, the wheel. Do not answer
to *imposter*, *pss*ting from behind cars. Ignore the way it whispers

from behind the mirror, or sneers in an interviewer's smile
as they slip a question mark after your name.

You try to seem relaxed, not pushed forward into this moment
by a thousand dry hands rough from factories and paddy fields

and postal rounds. As you shake hands on exit,
you think of the fists you've never had to form in pubs,

graffiti never scrubbed off your front door, nor shit,
nor brick or glass swept from your carpet. Still sometimes

the ground won't hold us. Uncles are flown back
in the night after fifty years on British soil, as if your family

are brown burrs picked off a white jumper one by one.
How would you survive if they came for you? Swelter in the heat,

lilt your English accent, don't flatten and comb your tongue
the way they learned to do it all those years ago

with a dream of gold streets and electric lights. In the dream,
their children live freely as kites, though our buoyancy

is terrifying without hands to hold us. Give us the strain
of the thread, though it hurts, and sometimes cuts the palm.

ICE-CREAM BOX OF FROZEN CURRY

Dear village leavers
Dear fortune seekers
Dear don't forget us
Dear whispered prayers
Dear check your papers
Dear three-week voyage
Dear Queen-saluting
Dear brylcreemed hair

Dear change your first name
Dear get to work
Dear roads and railways
Dear NHS
Dear filthy Paki
Dear bite your tongue
Dear keep your head down
Dear try your best

Dear sending for your wife and children
Dear colour riot flooding streets
Dear neighbours peeking through net curtains
Dear huddle in the winter sleet

Dear noses twitch at frying spices
Dear Southall for the best mangoes
Dear show the girls at school your mehndi
Dear Bhangra Baila Rock 'n' Roll

Dear ice-cream box of frozen curry
Dear tiny aunts with iron grip
Dear random portly shouting uncles
Dear grandmas wince at dodgy hip

Dear mothers at the cash and carry
Dear daughters always at the sink
Dear chubby sons stuffed with seconds
Dear father has another drink

Dear make-up practice after lights off
Dear boyfriend legs it out the back
Dear promise I was in the library
Dear shaving threading bleaching wax

Dear bragging round the kitchen table
Dear doctor lawyer engineer
Dear look at everything we gave you
Dear mother spilling ready tears

Dear load of strangers at the wedding
Dear spend the whole time on your phone
Dear don't know how to do the ritual
Dear feeling crowded and alone

Dear tongue is losing all the language
Dear stories melting into mist
Dear have to google wrapping saree
Dear still have no clue how to fit

Dear countries sinking underwater
Dear populations under threat
Dear clueless bhindi wearing ravers
Dear soon there will be nothing left

Dear elders shrinking into silence
Dear complicated tabla beat
Dear tell us of your fading memories
Dear show us how you find your peace

Dear give us tools for our tomorrow
Dear teach us all your ancient arts
Dear pass around the seed of kindness
Dear show us how to make it last

Dear Brick Lane, Bradford, Leeds and Hounslow
Dear Delhi, Dhaka, Colombo
Dear keep the conversation going
and make sure no one's on their own.

HOW NOT TO WRAP A SAREE
for Pooja Nansi

You stood at the ironing board for an age,
sailed that hot ship slowly over yards of copper silk,
fingers scanning the surface like a water-strider.

There is no time for such delicate handling as you hide
in the bathroom at your friend's wedding with a woman
you only met yesterday at the Mehndi, and now you're

trying to get each other dressed. The YouTube tutorials
have slipped down the back of your mind just when
you needed them, and it definitely doesn't look right:

bunches and gapes where a smooth plane of colour
should follow your flesh. You unravel and start again,
gather the warm spill of fabric in your hands and tuck,

wind and drape, teeth full of pins, securing pleats,
fingers at each others' shoulders and waists.
Hurry as the murmur of guests seeps under the door.

Though neither of you is sure you look better than a couple
of particularly opulent Egyptian mummies, you venture
into the room where your friend glitters in red georgette,

her dupatta encrusted with pearls, her wrists and ankles
a jangle of gold, sparkling eyes rimmed with black.
You hope no one will notice you clutch the bloody thing

Jasmine Cooray | 23

to yourself, its folds already escaping the waistband
like lava from a volcano. Your accomplice shuffles quickly
to the nearest chair, and as you clamber for a space,

conspicuously English: *terribly sorry, could I just?*
a woman turns her coiffed head and in her face you see
every aunt who knows this art like an alphabet,

every cousin whose hands could turn the ingredients
of body and garment into a woman who felt like,
and didn't just pass for, someone who belonged.

FAKE TAN

In the staff room before dinner rush, Sofia shoves
orange flesh into her waitress' shirt and apron.

I have half-shed my chef whites, one brown arm
sidetracked by texting, when—

Bitch, I spend hundreds of pounds on fake tan.
This could be anything; the tables she is late for,

the boyfriend who skulks outside at closing time
like an assassin, the lost baby, but for now,

my skin is the issue. I am boardrooms of men
deciding which way we should run for love,

always changing the rules. She tightens her bleached
ponytail in the mirror, throws a smile, sharp.

NASI LEMAK WITH THE ANCESTORS

Yong Ming is estranged – too flamboyant
for his rigid clan *but still*, he says, *we must take
care of them*. He places a teaspoon of coconut rice

on its small plate, a sliver of fried egg, a smear
of sambal. *Good thing they're not fussy!* he laughs,
sliding the dollhouse china onto its altar, where

incense wisps from foil wrapping. At restaurants,
polythene pouches emerge from his pockets,
doggy bags for generations of passed souls.

I imagine his cluster of white-haired relatives,
kneeling at a sky trapdoor, cloudy-eyed, gnarled
knuckles clutching canes, long grey beards,

tiny women with lined faces and crushed feet,
bickering in quick rasps, plucking at rice grains
with chopsticks. I think of my Aachi and Seeya.

Do they watch me from the afterlife, rub their hands
at New Year, its spread of red rice, pani, seeni sambol?
Do their faces fall when I lick my plate, leave them
  nothing?

ELDERS OF THE POT

They sit in a rainbow of re-used jam jars, watch
the traffic of the kitchen, hold proverb and gossip in
their gnarled shapes and powders. Every wooden spoon

is yellow to the neck. Turmeric, coriander, mustard seed
land on the heat of inherited pans, smoke their sour huck
into the corners of the house, leak under door frames.

They lodge, stubborn in curtain fibres, carpet, catch
the back of the throat when the chilli's capsaicin wakes,
beats its chest, a genie who gets too little sleep.

Some wait until the table to shock the soft palate.
Extract the debris piece by piece, pull cinnamon shards
from the pouch of a cheek, star anise, cardamom husks.

The trick is to act like it does not bother you, resisting
the fork, balling wet and dry between your fingers, copying
adults, learning to taste the notes that hum through veins.

You can smell it down the street, fenugreek and Impulse
fighting it out beneath your school uniform. If we lost our way,
still we could fumble back, follow those olfactory tones

until our noses found the door, the hob, the pot, the lid.
What is home but a map you don't need? You sneak a taste.
To know it's ready is the only language you have.

Jasmine Cooray

QUIET MEN

For solace, you nestle in broadsheets,
dank sheds full of home-brewed ale,
on allotments, thick fingers raking soil,

or surface to dispel a pub brawl
with a palm on the shoulder,
a whisper into a hot red ear.

Silence is something you walk,
yogic on its hot coals, your
breath slow through all that stings.

We flood our senses to avert
its heat, but you've walked
that narrow strip all our lives.

We walk across with you
from one edge to another,
learning to tread without fear.

I'M NOT GOING ANYWHERE
I PROMISE

you tell me, your arms around me like fleece.
I have done my best to harden against
all the love that came knocking, yet now
here you are, surrendering like a stranger
approaching the house of a ragged
woman with a rifle and a German Shepherd,
both hands open above your head.
You see her skinny frame, filthy nightdress
in the cold March light. You stand
steady in your jeans and brushed cotton shirt,
shoulders broad, eyes still and reassuring.
As I fill with dread of times to come
(maybe our flat, deserted, *I'm sorry*
on a paper bag; a hair on your jacket
too long to belong to either of us;
a red gingham tablecloth swept
to a crash of crockery; the back
of your head, becoming smaller), you remain,
still there at the gate. The sky is darkening:
you have turned your collar up, and now
I notice I am crying but your arms
have not moved from around me.
My belief, a small fire burning
in an attic in a ghost town.

WORLD OF WILDFLOWERS

ELEGY FOR A WEDDING

Our lives set the scene for love / not meant to be /
more like *the conditions are ideal* / rainbow from light and
rain / two mouths meeting along one strand of spaghetti /
hearts open enough / ground fallow / tender / laughter
like confetti / you sat through shite poetry / took me
seriously / ripped the piss too / reminding each other /
how to let love in

A ring sizer in your drawer / your jeweller / father / said
yes / you knew I would too / my mother makes dresses
/ your brother takes photos / I imagined our nieces
crowned in garlands / our missing parents hovering near us
like smoke / we talked about a cliff house / a cat called
Imhotep / years brimming with staves and stanzas /
a school / sea swimming / dreams of shore / bluster and
bonfires / wedding a festival of artists and healers /
you were harvest time

Our bright autumn day / never came / not that kind /
you left in September / orange leaves and golden sun /
you revered warm palettes / I dressed for your funeral like
it was a wedding / our friends and families on pews / at
least they saw us together once / I spoke / vows disguised
as eulogy / the groom dressed in a box / the bride in a
veil of steel / don't let the tears come / for they will wash
away our dreams

WORLD OF WILDFLOWERS
for Will

A packet of wildflower seeds sits
on the mantelpiece, and in it is you.

You would find nature's splashes of colour
on any street, stop to greet the tiniest bloom

as if it were a miniature king, your face lit,
laughter bursting from you like a firework.

This was the richness of how you lived,
and how you live still. Lately we seem

to find flowers in unexpected places:
sunflowers blooming from club speakers,

lavender sprouting between piano keys,
a black cat collared with daisies

and when we, who miss you, embrace,
petals explode between our chests.

Your world was a garden in which to grow
love. You left it open for us to walk in.

THE FIELDS

He seemed to be there, then, though I had
no language for it, no dogma or formula
to explain the feeling that a man who had died
was somehow here again, waving, but more
than this, was all around me. In the morgue,
I had thought suddenly *you need to be set free*,
and sung a love song over the body. Now I looked out
on the fields by his house: grass, golden, blustering,
September sun shimmering and molten
and thought *this was your favourite kind of light*.
Strong wind pushed against my body, gathered
up my parts and placed them back with me,
tidying what had dispersed when I shattered
upon losing him, when I wanted to float away
and join him, in the sky and the wind and the fields.

INHERITANCE

I wake to this gift: a song of love so fierce
and melodic I feel it swell like a wave.

I heard you hum this all the time
but it's only now that the tune sticks,

circling above me like a hanging mobile as I sleep.
I hum it as I dress, wash the dishes.

I do not know what greater gift there is
to give someone than unshatterable faith

in their own worth: like a safe filled with gold
in an otherwise obliterated building.

BLESSING

Now time leads me carefully through daily toast,
washing machine rotations. My clothes
are so clean and pressed now. Their order
can be restored over and over, but ours cannot.

I've decided not to join you, so then here it is,
the future, its possibilities like hands
outstretched in a stadium. I confess, I want
to grasp them: to feel again the warmth of skin,

the shifting weight on a mattress,
the taste of beer on another mouth, all
the not-knowings that harden into knowing
like cooling lava. I want before, but if not,

give me the mess of learning another's language
the way I learned yours, wove it into my ways –
and I speak more than me, now. I speak us,
but to pronounce it properly

I need joy, my love. Will you grant me that now,
as you did? Will you watch and help me
tilt my chin up, face skywards, scanning,
willing the clouds to break again?

SONG FOR ABSENT LOVES

When I could not touch your face, my love,
with its soft lines and history,
I ran my fingers over the leaves and bark
of the trees in the local streets.

When I could not feel your gaze, my love,
washing over me like bliss,
I stood still in the sun and the winter breeze
each whisper and ray like a kiss.

When your arms were not here for holding, my love,
and I whimpered at night like a dog
I packed myself in with pillows, snug,
like a parcel of china pots.

When you didn't pick up the phone, my love,
and there was no one to hear my heart,
I told everyone else I loved them, dear,
and serenaded my potted plants.

'Though you could not take me to dance, my love,
couldn't twirl me in clubs and halls,
I still dressed up in lipstick and heels, my love,
jived alone with a glitter ball.

When you could not be here to cook for, my love,
your plate filled with flavour and cheer,
I left cakes on the neighbours' doorsteps,
filled my freezer enough for a year.

My heart is a bath overfilling, my love,
and it needs to flow somewhere new,
and for now, that somewhere is everywhere:
and everywhere, somewhere, is you.

THE CALL

He has hands like Shiva: one in the navy change belt,
one pointing at avocados, crackly-skinned cantaloupes,

other hands weighing, bagging, pinching the corners
of brown paper bags, flipping them sealed and taut.

Over commuters scurrying homeward the voice launches
like a whale plume arching over waves – *Banana banana!*

Lovely bit o' cherry, each phrase coming round as if
unclaimed on a luggage carousel, a voice perfect

for shifting goods before the sun punches entry wounds
into peaches or slackens each grape to an old balloon.

He takes an *alright dahlin*, serves it to me with a wink
and two punnets of strawberries. It is late in the day.

On the kitchen counter, the haul will reveal pink slime,
bruised berries weeping under more pert candidates,

but it's the call, not the fruit, that draws me: past
the supermarket; its disinfected leaves in cellophane,

earthless spuds, and the quack of self-service machines,
churning punters through on their cold flat song.

PACK EVERYTHING DOWN

vacuum seal it, push it
somewhere deep, lightless.

Others exhale with relief:
open wounds are hard to look at.

Become neat and shiny
like a column of pennies.

The slightest movement,
and you spill everywhere.

PORTOBELLO DUSK

As we walk through the manicured public gardens
where fountains gush from stone fish, I don't pause
to revere swallows scribbling cursive loops against

pink cloud, or linger by the small Italian restaurant
with its wine bottles collared in wax. I haven't worn the dress
that cinches me to hourglass, left the red lipstick

in the drawer: I beat loudly enough as it is, friend, though
I pretend to forget, like a creature born wild and brought
to cage or glass. We were hungry here, once, hands

everywhere, evenings swept clear like countertops,
all other plans clattering to the floor. Now we ignore
the bar that emptied around us, the wall that left itself

in the back of my coat. I don't need to point out the stops.
You know them, your face in profile all night as if blinkered
from the look in my eyes you remember not being able to
  refuse.

STORYTELLER

During silent nights I tell myself the story
of his hands on my body, but it wasn't love.

It wasn't love when he zipped open
his pale sternum and told me where it hurt,

where the mewling howled from.
His sweat and tears on my hands

turned silver by the moon
that blazed through the skylight

but lying under those glass-paned stars
with him wasn't it. I collected all the milk

of the light and his skin like rainwater in drought,
a drought where love was once flowing

its wide river. I tell myself this story
of leaving thirst behind, and I tell it well,

my heart like a child who needs to hear
it before she can sleep, to wake again.

TAWNY OWL

I heard you through the bathroom window,
silver-milk sound like a bubble of moonlight
flowing through the dark. Wonder at your call,

so far from woodland or fields with scurrying voles.
I found you the next day on the pavement,
not the closed-limb shroud of a swaddled child:

not just an owl sleeping too deeply and fallen,
but crumpled by a wall like a man passed out, drunk.
I carried you into the church gardens by your feet,

later buried you beneath a tree under cover of dark,
hacked inexpertly at the London clay with a child's
gardening spade, dug a small bed to tuck you into.

Your soft body lay along my wrist to the elbow
like a sleeping baby. There were loosenesses
inside you, where there should be tension,

where the breaks were. One wing still outstretched.
I folded it into you, broken umbrella, for comfort,
your round eyes closed as if in prayer, and packed

the cold earth on top, no time to flinch from worms
or woodlice, hurrying, aware of how this all might look.
And then, my love, I cried and sang for you all night,

tried to find the silver-milk in my voice for you,
magnificent beast, custodian of the dark.
Sleep, wild thing. I wish we could tell your family.

Instead, this flimsy human gesture, apology
for our fast machines, who steal your swoop
and catch, your mottled umber, your gold.

DREAM POSTERS

My insides were plastered up and down
with dreams like posters of childhood heroes

two hooks for house keys
                        coral reef honeymoon

do you think this needs salt darling
                                breastfeeding lullabies

Bless your spy-hole imaginings, the sky says,
there's so much you can't see,

can't know which energetic stranger
will suddenly pull you from a queue,
salsa with you on a bridge,
which frothing waters you will kayak down,
which land you will come to call home.

Oh the courage, I know, is costly.
To clear space on those walls,
feel the coldness of the pale squares beneath.

But sweetheart, who knows what
all those dreams were really like in person?

SWEET MILK

i.

In the story corner, giant beanbags and bright shelves
stacked with *Spot The Dog*, *The Very Hungry Caterpillar*,

is a pair of laddered stockings in wide-fit loafers.
Yes – you know that BHS skirt, and the voice,

slow and patient, though next to her sits a different
child moulding his mouth around the word sounds,

squinting as she points out each letter. You, frizzy pigtails,
buzz with surprise, a small bird suddenly sharing a nest

with thirty other chicks squalling to feed on that laugh,
those reassuring woollens. You colour harder, curl

the page with red crayon, hot little face wondering
how much of the day's worm will be left for you.

ii.

She was married off quick, Ma says, tracking her mind
over Grandma, hustled onto a ship bound for England,

a soldier's Polish genes budding in her belly. Four more
by the naval officer-come-bricklayer, a quiet man

with tobacco fingers and anchors faded to duck egg
on forearms burnished under Sussex sun. And Ma,

brought up alongside all the same, though she lacked
that signature chin and thin lips to mark her his.

My real dad must be dead now, she says, imagining
a grave marked in Polski, a cluster of half-siblings

laying a table with sausage, potatoes, beetroot stew,
steaming pierogi sifted one by one from the pot.

Now his story moulders in the skull of a woman whose lips
wax and wane, her words slipping behind dense cloud,

skin creased like a letter that has been re-read, folded,
pressed in a secret place. Somewhere in her is a name.

iii.

Ma pores over her collection of stones,
picked not for prettiness but function.

Shards of flint — Mesolithic, she thinks — borers,
scrapers that a layperson might overlook,

shake from a shoe after walking the dog,
some small as fingernails. I love to watch

her honour each stone blade, imagine her
treading footpaths with a searchlight gaze,

seeing fires, lean men in skins and furs
striking rock to rock. She plucks each wedge

of planet from anonymity like a music mogul
rocketing a busker to celebrity, then brings

them home, cushioned between soft fingertips,
panics if one escapes into a pile of newspapers

or the cave of a boot. I watch her attention
bathe like spring light; watch her wash soil

from these countless relics, turn each one
over at the kitchen sink's cold tap, then dry

carefully with tissue in the clefts and creases,
tending to them as if they were her own.

iv.

The year candles were bought from occult shops
where glowing staff seemed not to walk but glide,

velvet-skirted and jingling from counter to shelf,
I swung pentagrams to ward against heartbreak,

acne, the bully in the school courtyard. A ring binder
overflowed with spells in purple ink, all the magic

a fledgeling witch might need. Once I found the folder
missing, and downstairs, my mother's finger poised

on one page, the other hand brandishing a black candle,
her eyes wild, triumphant as a gold-hunter, proclaiming

I'm going to cast a spell on that arsehole, Tony Blair!
A child making a sword of a stick imagines anything

to be possible. Two million marched that summer,
and at home this woman, godless since convent nuns

caned all the worship from her, muttered incantations
over a newspaper photo, the toothy grin splodged with wax.

v.

When that sweet milk starts to dull on the tongue,
a painting slowly fading by a window,

there is the mother of your friend doing 'Night Fever'
in her kitchen or draped like Dietrich over an armchair,

kohl pulsing through cigarette smoke. She calls
you *darling* as you've never heard it before,

remaking you delicious, a summer cherry bursting
between teeth. One night in her beach house, she feeds

you and your friend LSD in a sugar cube, and the rain
courses upwards, water a runaway

with a change of heart, flocking back to cloud.
Better than getting it elsewhere she husks in the room

next door, while you take turns doing forward rolls
across the carpet. You didn't know love came

in this shape, could twist its hips in a figure
of eight or smell of an endless balmy Friday night.

Tanned diva, bra-less in summer linen, driving you
to the edge of the cliff, daring you to look over.

vi.

My mother adjusts my sister's breast
so the baby can drink. Her soft fingers,
lined from years in dish soap, lightly pull
at the doughy flesh, moving the nipple.
They are like one being: murmur
to one another, to the child, a breeze
flowing through different rooms of a house.
I watch from the plastic chair, my womb full
of words. I do not know what else it can host,
whether I will walk the road to that place
of soft skulls and sacrifice, where a tender
language is spoken, and where my mother,
her touch soothing and certain and magical,
is still a cool balm in the fever of our lives.

YEARS THAT ASK QUESTIONS AND YEARS THAT ANSWER

THE FALLING
after Bowie

It began with one patch, a bare circle
like a pale coin, the sun beating down, scorching.

Nobody thought much of it, but then came more.
Wind flew through the gaps like someone whistling
through teeth, and there was the cold, rain,
each drop acute as a root canal.

When the surface started to resemble
an inverse leopard, others started to
scramble for remedies, ointments
and injections, chants, incantations,
but the illness tearing through the body
was too strong for medicine or prayer.

When there was nothing left,
what remained was a smooth skull, cool,
like a planet distant from a star.

The world as I knew it had died, bore
a new one, open, open to the sky.

A TASTE OF THE END

At the woman with no hair, he can't stop looking,
pinched between chopsticks of fear and desire.

He imagines tumours rippling quickly through her
like drops of ink in water, like billowing fungus,

wants her more, to claim her last sweetness
as if she is a final glut of fruit, on the turn.

We clamour for sex when death is near
though she is dying no more than he is,

every cell's bloom and decay like flowers
folding themselves into the mulch of the body.

Makes you grateful to be alive he thinks
except he isn't, just curious about the burn

of a sparkler hissing out on his tongue:
he wonders if fucking her will jolt him awake,

like a head pulled from a basin of water.
If he got closer he would hear a drum

warning off those bored with living,
beating loudly in her veins.

AGAINST THE GRAIN

When my niece is born, my mother calls
up the stairs to me *better get one in quick.*

Time pushes me over the summit of Thirty,
and everyone panics as politely as they can

about having their faces filled with dust
when I hit those menopausal plains.

They bleat *you'd be beautiful pregnant*
as if pregnant is a dress to be tried on

but I wouldn't get to take off motherhood.
Little one, be born from a sure belly.

Maybe I will meet you somewhere;
as a student, a godchild, a baby gurgling

on a bus, and my free heart will give you
so much more than if you were mine.

SWEET PRINCE
for Albie Hueston

And then there was your laughter
full of stars, lifting me out of myself
like someone trapped in a well.

If not for you, how would I have known
club queues, pumping bass, glitter's
indelible trail, or the sweet love of men

who wanted my body for nothing
but a dance, a sweaty cheek kiss,
to dole out *you're beautiful* as they passed.

Men heaving in a room without threat,
leading me through the night without threat,
spooning me in their bed without threat,

coming so close but never breaking
the membrane, never spilling me
like a fox lapping at a hen's egg

and you, all cheekbones and jokes,
carving out each step, holding my hand
as we learned how to be queer and free,

how my heart leapt for you, and how
you caught it, held it up to the light
like a moonstone, *see, see how you glow.*

BADONK

The marble goddesses at Neasden Temple
move their hips along infinity signs
as if someone snuck psilocybin into my coffee.
Warmth moves my body without music,
syrup in my uterus, silk around my waist.
I am mountain range. I am rolling wave.
What a bloody shame: all those years trying
to carve everything down lean and narrow
like a cylinder of kebab meat and here,
bellies, thighs, bulging soft and lush.
Later at the party, where normally I'd shuffle,
swaddled, awkward, avoiding arm movements,
I let the flesh move without me, as it does
if the gods have been generous when serving.

ALWAYS THE QUIET ONES
after Mary Oliver

I cannot claim to be good.
Yes, there were birthday cakes,
batter lovingly smoothed in the tin,
letters many pages long. I've sat
in hospital waiting rooms, tipped buskers,
watered plants. In a murder trial
the press would write 'not the type',
or 'pulled the wool over our eyes', my smile
accruing a horror-film glaze
in photographs. How many times
have I imagined explosions bursting
through all that layered rock?
Lord knows I long to be a cunt out loud.
Then would the dark still curdle
as it does, stuck in that cave, growing,
mutating, desperate to escape?

MAKING AMENDS

The ex arrives at the small anonymous cafe
neither of you knew before. After the small talk

you fumble around in the past for old ugly things
trapped like fossils. Slowly the table is cluttered

with memories that sit awkwardly among the cups
and sugar like children ushered forward by parents

to apologise for a smashed window. As you lay
them out, the words you practised threaten to bitter

your throat like bile, though now each *I'm sorry*
that leaves your mouth feels hollow as a bubble.

The ex looks at you with something between sorrow
and rage because she was just fine no thanks to you,

didn't bank on being dragged back in time by the hair
and there is no guide for this bit, for when

the thorns lie bloody between you, the places
they were buried in stinging like goodwill.

THE WELL
for Ruby

A woman sees how tightly
her friend's smile is hoisted up,

watches the shoulders slowly bow,
feels her step carefully around him

when speaking, arriving late to coffee,
jumpy when the phone rings,
                              rings.

She knows where her friend has gone
but neither says a word.

From inside the well, the other
can hear a voice, a song

like a rope ladder into the dark.
They stay like that for days,
                              weeks,

one bent over the side, calling,
one building up the courage to leave,

each listening for the other's voice,
each praying the other will not give up.

ALL THE TREES HOLDING HANDS UNDER THE EARTH
after Shoshana Anderson

Light lands on me: you feel it through your roots
even when you are in shadow,
or fungus has reduced you to mottled bark,
flaking, the curl of chalky leaves, arthritic.

There's a subtle electrical crackle
as if the pinky finger of my history
hooks into yours, somewhere
deep among mulch, spores, insect eggs,
sliver of a seed's pale foot pushing down.

Though I can't see where we are touching
I choose to assume we are,
or why would it feel like this, stranger,
when you sit down and speak?

As if I'm looking into my own face.
you open the window of your life
and a breeze blows through mine,
shivers through my outermost parts.

BAD HOSTING

The cup is right in front of you, and the sink
three metres away, but that three metres,

even the thought of it, grinds you
into mush like a pestle.

When your heart is clogged like the gut
of a dead whale choked with plastic,

make the tasks small. I mean small like a breath,
small like maybe today isn't the day for dying.

Imagine another chair at the table, where something
you've not yet considered might sit.

Look, I might sound unreasonable,
but if you're willing to keep hosting the past

could we also wipe off a plate in case the future
arrives, bringing baklava, kissing you

on the cheek – just in case her hand on yours
feels like full-bloom peony and smells of vanilla?

You might have to wash the cup – it'll feel
wrong to serve tea from a half-clean jam jar.

There we go – sponge on the side, love.
Squeeze it in your palm like a stress ball,

the stale liquid reeking. Wring it out,
don't leave it to rot. There's life in it yet.

YEARS THAT ASK QUESTIONS AND YEARS THAT ANSWER
after Zora Neale Hurston

Some years asked *what are you made of,*
and you started getting out cupcakes and bunting
and they shook their head and said *no, really,*
and you curtseyed in a nurse's uniform and halo,
and they sighed and said *yes but what else,*
and you felt around in there and said *ok, fire,*
and nailbombs and rubble, and they said *good what else,*
and you said *a scream filling the universe,*
and before they could ask again you coughed up
parachutes and kaleidoscopes and carnival outfits
and panthers and peacocks and flying fish,
and spider webs holding cannonballs
and mountains and rivers and tree roots
and then the years answered by rising,
breaking through the roof like Alice, a giant
treading the earth, then curling up in the ocean
to rest from all the work of those question years,
hip curving above the waves, a new country.

ACKNOWLEDGEMENTS

Firstly, thank you to Amy and Jake at Bad Betty for receiving this book in your hearts and believing in it. Particular thanks to Amy for your sharp and kind editorial eye, I am so grateful for your tenderness and your faith in 'less is more'. Thank you also for your striking and thoughtful cover design.

Thank you to Spread the Word for supporting my writing over many years. Thank you to Mimi Khalvati for her stellar poem feedback as part of the BBC Performing Arts Fund Scheme.

Thank you to the National University of Singapore and The Arts House, Singapore, for providing a new context of experience and friendship.

Thank you to Anthony Joseph, in whose workshop 'Inventory' was first drafted. And to both Anthony and to Salena Godden for so generously taking the time to read this work and share their estimations of it.

Thank you to Nik Perring, in whose workshop 'The Falling' was drafted.

Thank you to the Southbank Centre for commissioning 'Ice-Cream Box of Frozen Curry' for the Alchemy Festival, 2015.

To David, Loz, Tim, Liz, Luvain, Anna, James and Shay, Patrick (RIP), and Louise, thank you for welcoming me into the family of those who love Will and grieving him with me.

To the teachers and supporters in my therapy community, including: Roz Carroll, Shoshi Asheri, Robert Downes, Janice Acquah, Chance Czyzselska, Amabel Sutters, Emilyn Claid, Felicia Smith-Kleiner, Mick Langan, thank you for blowing the embers of my creative voice when they were low, and keeping me steady.

Thank you to my immediate and extended family for being there and supporting me not just in showing interest in my work, but in allowing me to not feel alone when the living was hard.

To Leila, Miriam, Kayo, Sarah, Mina, Ruby, Farrah, Akwasi, Brett, Claudia, Joanne, Rosanna, Lucy, Anjali: having you as my friends gives me solace, encouragement, jokes, stability, relief, breakfast, somewhere to cry, and more places to repot my heart into. I am composite of your love.

To everyone who ever replied with something lovely on my Tinyletter mailout list or who shared any of my poems on: you made a huge difference to my confidence, thank you.

To the poetry community at large: thank you for giving me spaces to speak, still being there and celebrating my work, and reminding me what poetry is for.

To the ancestors who are here while they're not: Taraknath Upali Cooray, Jessica Warnakula Cooray, John Frederick Cooray, Anne-Marie Huiveneers, Susan Hensel, and the countless unnamed, I carry you with me in all your love and complexity, may I keep remembering how (and why) to live, speak and be free.

To Will, as you shine through dappled light and throb through bright flowers and whisper to me from beyond: thank you for remaking me a woman who knows the value of love. Somewhere you're laughing.